PLAYING HOUSE

For Dave

Katherine STANSFIELD

PLAYING HOUSE

Penarth, 9/7/17.

To Dorothy,

with my best
wishes - flying
poem still to
come!

SEREN

Seren is the book imprint of
Poetry Wales Press Ltd.
57 Nolton Street, Bridgend, Wales, CF31 3AE
www.serenbooks.com
Twitter: @SerenBooks
facebook.com/SerenBooks

ISBN: 978-1-78172-193-3
e-book: 978-1-78172-195-7
Kindle: 978-1-78172-194-0

A CIP record for this title is available from the British Library.

The publisher acknowledges the financial assistance of the Welsh Books Council.

Cover: Heather Landis/Illustration Ltd.

Printed in Bembo by Bell & Bain Ltd, Glasgow

Author's Website: katherinestansfield.blogspot.co.uk

Contents

O bees of Rhode Island

You're bolshie in morning hover, smug humming
zip tours of roses, those puckered-up girls,
while the pool's unblinking eye gives back
your stateliness, your striped I'm-great-liness.
Hop a jig along, stop –
take the measure of after-margarita me,
bare-legged, still drunk in the gazebo.
Why must you kamikaze for accidental grazes
and sheer not-knowing swats?
Why must you threaten me
with your terrible kiss? Know this:
when I am savaged by Maine flies
and ants swoon in the sweet relish,
I'll praise you and your raffish pride.
Behold my obeisance, o bees of Rhode Island.
You are all propulsion, miracle,
and the goodness of the day.

Training event

A woman who sits too close to me
and talks over other people
is now sitting too close to me
and talking over other people
to inform me that a blue tit flew
inside the building earlier today.

She tells me she followed shouts down
the corridor past open doorways giving
windows giving trees and found it stressed
on a shelf so she *sshhed* its quake until
it went stiff with shock but then
she didn't want to let go because
it was beautiful struck dumb.

The manager gives her a 'for God's sake'
look because he's ready to tell us about
effective communication in the workplace
and this woman is going on and on
as she's always going on and on
about the bird. I worry he thinks
I'm talking to her when she's talking to me

and I worry about the bird which for all I know
is in the woman's handbag at her feet
where it might wake at any moment, free
itself in a panicked flap and bang
my glasses or wet its wings
on my eyes while I scream and scream
into the lino's linty static.

I put up my hand and ask the manager
if there will be a PowerPoint slide
on how to effectively tell this woman
to leave me and the birds alone.

Africa on BBC One

I see now, East African Shoebill, that you
are the true face of my bird fear.
David Attenborough may laud

your survival in shrinking marsh
but I know you're a dodo
gone bad, a malicious sock puppet

with inappropriate legs. I'm not surprised
when one of your chicks kills the other
while I'm eating my spaghetti bolognaise,

watching. You see me, fork raised, appalled
and your Stanley knife mouthpiece flaps
into close up. I press a cushion to my face

but you knock it aside to pluck out my eyes
while David moves on to the parties
rhinos throw by night.

The woman on my National Library
of Wales library card

Her mouth says it all —
slack as a jellyfish. They made her

stand against the wall
with no time to pose or comb

the seagulls from her hair,
no time to dig her smile

from pockets of sand.
The sea fret foaming at her hems

thickened once inside the dusty air
that seeps from books. See, she's ghosting

under the card's laminated skin. Almost
gone. She fogged the enquiry desk too.

The attendant lost his hands
in the mist, hence the wonky

shot. She's looking at a horizon
beyond the frame. I can't meet

her salt-stiff eye which asks
for silence from the waves

as if such a gift could be given.
She doesn't get out much now for fear

of mackerel following her home
and wheezing to death in the road,

of mullet in the bath again.
Her doorstep is crunchy with limpets.

Can I take her something back?
She likes romance, set far inland.

To my cat camped
by the washing machine

That shrew has sailed.
What you can smell
is its week-old fear
and the scrap of chorizo
I dropped last night
and accidently pushed
right under the drum
with a wooden spoon
when I tried to save it.
Tough luck, kiddo.
We all have our losses.

Telescope

How far is it? From here
craters are like fingerprints
until the Circle Line shakes
and smudges the moon.

So we wait, rest our eyes, sip tea
until we can blink through Stockwell's
neon aurora. Taking turns, we slide

past one another in planetary intimacy,
our orbits not determined by grand design
but balcony railings, tomato plants.

The terminus comes into focus
when I'm not looking,
better seen without glasses:

that sharp line between
the face the moon shows us
and the one turned away.

I stay so long at the glass my tea cools
to clouds. When I queue for a cup
in a few days' time
a hundred miles west

I'll see news of a dead girl, shot
in a corner shop, on a corner not far
from here. What's she doing now
as we squint to see the moon?

In the hot darkness of the earth
the last tube clatters strangers home.
They doze, read, check their watches
and the moon wobbles back to a smear.

The untraceables

In dumb night the freaks
have snarled across

the sea, Spitfires lost
to weather reports. Sisters

of shriek, these bulb–
eaters batter a morning

raw. Sudden bluster,
shingle howl and shin

whip mass rooftops, skit–
tering fingers prise

slates, send flick knives
into scalps below. In

the roar I whisper *faster,*
girls, faster faster.

A35

I liked the dragon. You say it was predictable.
The woman in the red Fiesta is making a U-turn at the crossing.
We're on the other side of the road, talking about the film
and about narrative time, how the prequel we've just seen,
based on a book written first but filmed last in the series, fits –
or doesn't – with the old films. I can't explain
what I mean but it's something to do with expanding
the timeframe of the original film (and the book) that was really
second though it came first, and how the way they almost fit
together is satisfying. Not quite right but right still
and then the Fiesta hits the cyclist and he's lying
in the road and you're shouting and there's no time only
cars pulling over in front of us, the pulse of indicators,
and the Fiesta's main beam lighting the scene.

I didn't see you, the woman shouts at the cyclist. I didn't see you.

We're near Axminster when it begins to rain.

Anniversary voyage

I blew the year's holiday budget and sold
the wife's jewellery for the fare. Ten per cent off
because I'm family helped but we've debts now.
My daughter's ballet lessons have stopped.

No, I never knew Granddad. A drunk who beat
his kids, by all accounts, but he drowned
on the most famous ship ever to sink
so I'm here to pay my respects. The decks

are crammed with us. See the woman by the lifeboat?
She's second cousin of a potwash and the man
with a map of Nova Scotia's certain he lost someone.
At dinner I sit with a couple of buffs:

she collects washed-up buttons and her husband
watches. He says he likes them stopped at the sinking.
My wife? She's at home, eating beans on toast
and working extra shifts while I'm lording it

at the captain's table. Watch me take a replica knife
to my salmon and mousseline sauce, dissect my squab,
souse my salad with champagne. I wolf the last supper
on genuine plates, admire myself in a period spoon.

Tomorrow we'll sail to the spot and sing a hymn
to mark a century since she went down, to the minute.
The captain will drop a wreath and I'm hoping for ice
for the snaps. I want to lean over

and see myself in the water. I'll picture falling into
darkness, the cold, my scream swallowed by the sea.
When the cameras are rolling I'll climb the rail
and jump into that wonderful night, into history.

Missing:

You're everywhere. In my inbox when I get to work, on Twitter, on Facebook: someone else's friend shared and shared again. Missing. Have you seen. Please share. Missing.

You're everywhere. In the post office, the doctor's, the butcher's, the baker's, the train station, the toy shop, the sex shop, the phone box, the estate agent's, the cafes, the squash court, the empty shops, the nearly re-opened shops.

You're everywhere. On lampposts, in bus shelters, on boarded-up doorways. Carried in taxi windows, on the dashboards of vans, in handbags. As I walk home I see people putting the flyers under windscreen wipers and I want to ask if there's news, then I remember that I don't know you. We've never met.

But after today I'm sure I've seen you, been just behind you, just before you, maybe queuing at the same bar, waiting for the same bus. Today I've seen you leaning against a kitchen counter, a little shy in shirt and tie. I've seen you in close up on the sofa, laughing and looking away. The photos have you safe indoors, the frames keeping you still, where we can see you. You are on my doormat when I get home.

You're everywhere, I say, as I lay you out on my kitchen table. You're in every place we've looked so how did you disappear? Where did you go after you got your chips and slipped from CCTV's unmoving eye? You're everywhere, I say, but that's better than the nowhere of unlit streets on a drunk night out, better than the waiting sea beyond. This poem cannot bring you back from that, although it has brought you here, onto this page. I will write this and then recycle you. There's nothing else that I can do.

No room at the inn

All the animals in the animal basket
wanted to go: Stegosaurus,
polar bears, Lego dog.
We let in a camel and a donkey
only on sufferance. They watched
from the back, blocked by pandas.

The crib was crammed: shoe box
size, wooden, cotton wool snow
glued to the tin-foiled top. Our desert
in the dining room was cold.
Stacks of straw kept everyone warm
but because we wouldn't do wisps
we lost baby Jesus early on.

The angel with a 'gloria' sash lashed
to the stable door was meant to be
ever-descending. We spent Christmas
knocking her off on the way
to the kitchen and having to rehang
her chipped china robe.

Each night we said sleep tight, Lego dog,
sleep tight, panda family, sleep tight,
Joseph and Mary, but when
we'd climbed the wooden hill
disaster struck our Bethlehem: the cat –
crib-fancier, straw-lover, jealous, always,
of religious icons – pushed
herself in, knocked everyone out.

Swine song

Pig's eyes had long been clouds
that threatened rain but when Lickpan
sparked his kindest knife the storms

blew out. Pig was pleased. He'd been low
these fetid summer nights, lonely
but for hawthorn and shy rabbits

since full moon Friday last,
when pig forgot what beast he was
and clamped his big grin

round his brother's neck, smiling
until it snapped.
Pig took his separation hard

but once he'd got the taste I couldn't trust
that charming curly tail. Poor chap
sighed until his spots fell off, quivered

his bristles to fluff. His night-time cries
could pare the hardest heart. I thought it best
to send for Lickpan and I'm glad

now that Pig's pain has gone. My love
has salted down the other cuts. Please start –
this chop's sweeter for its sadness.

Hares I have seen

The first crashed a fence in a field near Shrewsbury.
It was after lunch of lamb slow-roasted for a night
and a day, its grease still slick on my fingers when she broke
from the stubble. I forgot her later when I sat on a swing
and cried. That time it was for loneliness.

The second raced the train taking me to Edinburgh.
A break in the hedge revealed for a blink the reach
of her stride, the gathering of feet beneath belly before
the hedge snapped back. I forgot her later when I cried
into moussaka. That time it was for loneliness and drink.

The third hung from a hook in a butcher's in Ludlow.
Her legs were primly crossed and bound, her head
shrouded in muslin but there was no mistaking
the checked spring, the white flag beneath her tail.
She was too big that close though her ears were shorn
because what good are ears when paying by weight?
I couldn't forget her but by then I'd given up crying.

That night she was in the mirror. She pulled off the muslin
to parade her holed skull, rolled her pale eyes and –
                                        worst of all –
flashed a stiff grin of yellow teeth bared to chip any dish
I'd try to jug her in. I went to bed without flossing. I cried
into dry fur. That time it was for everything.

Portrait of Guy Pearce as a hare

not about ears   rather harishness
of gait: lanky
quicksilver flit
          to the form

he is grace lollop
the shot   all haunch springing
                              bravura
then shanks   panic

jaw slung   sadface til
grin sickles   pulling
faces   pretending levret

see it? just
me   well
box gentle   guy
              you bloody beauty

Relic

One of John Lennon's teeth is expected to make
£10,000 when it is auctioned next month.
                    BBC News, 19th October 2011

In the kitchen, bracing
his pain between the table
and the stove, he tore
tooth from gum

with a wet crunch, gave it,
bloody, *as a souvenir,*
and walked out beyond
decay.

After fifty years it looks
like forgotten popcorn
or a knot of Wrigley's
chewed past stretch.

Only the root suggests
it was once nerved-in
to a jaw that tenderised
Lennon's meat.

What will you do with it?

Keep it in a matchbox
in a jam jar in a football sock
underneath the bed, warmed
each night knowing it's there.

Ask your stunned dentist
to replace a molar so you
can share that grin
with the bathroom mirror.

Plant it behind the shed,
marked by bamboo,
and watch for bone
to break the soil.

Or, on days your own tune
won't play, put it to your ear
like a shell, and hear
the long dead croon:

love, love me do.

Trevithick

Not the genius from a county thick
with clever dicks: Davy, Gurney, Cookworthy.
Not the giant whose strong steam
made hearts and engines race
then explode. Not the inventor
of the storage heater, the reaction turbine,
the one who raised wrecks from the seabed
and when he wasn't paid let them sink.

Our Trevithick came down with a third
it was whispered, took to teaching science
like a man condemned. Bald and furious,
fat-collared suit and fatter tie beneath
the pristine lab coat, a slab
of signet ring on a hand twitching
to let us have it.
                        I'd get top grades
he told my parents, if only I'd
pipe up, stop hiding under the desk
when Bunsens were lit.
                        I wasn't one
for melting biros into brittle swans
or sparking battery clips with drawing pins.
I wasn't one for weighing the Greek
of equations and shouting out
Sir, it's speed, it's distance, it's a positive charge

because I saw the pistons working his jaw
and the furnace stoked in his cheeks,
because I knew the Puffing Devil's
pressure gauge always cracked.

Cream teas, Sunday

The four o'clock rush stampedes in at three
to besiege us, heathens sweating scones
for Sunday's sore visitor gods. Raging and raw
we keep out cats, flies, the customers
still crash right through with sugar in their eyes.
Quick – lay your hands on the cream
to banish mould and I'll speak in tongues
of jam. Hell opens to burn the slovenly
and pour forth fruitcake and smoke.
I weep into my apron. There's no change
or tips. Tea cosies drown in Lapsang floods,
exhausted pots shatter and teaspoons bolt,
menus make for the door and coffee jars
revolt. You spread the charm like soft butter
on a split and I'll give sticky grace on not quite
clean plates. Will that appease them?
Our fake accents turn with the milk
come six. Prayers pass in a kettle's pant,
returning to water and air: tomorrow
please rain, please rain, please rain.

To her, waiting

There must have been a row, some great betrayal.
No one remembers now. You said nothing, just packed
orange squash and a sheep's skull in a Tesco bag

and hid. When the men broke for crib you slunk
from the farmhouse, kept low past the barn
because the horses would call you back

or give you up with a snicker. You never trusted
their stillness, knowing the bolt lay hidden
in the whites of their eyes. Too many falls.

You stopped at the cattle grid, twelve rust-pocked bars
to keep you in and wild ponies out.
They waited on the other side, backs to the rain,

making your heart cha-cha-cha with worry-love.
Their numb flanks found an echo in the fat
of your haunch, the slap of your rump; you dripped

with them in the downpour, somehow inside
their grease-warm skins. Beyond their huddle
the moor – overgrazed and underloved

by sheep and motorbikes. Dead gorse laid
a maze with the prize of somewhere else,
somewhere that might be better, somewhere

you cried for in the bath. But the ponies
didn't move because you couldn't move
to break their lonely circle. Your need left

potholes to be filled by rain. When I came back
I felt you there, even in fresh water, still waiting
for your chance to run, no – to walk – away.

Soundings

My voice is engine house and saffron.
The man in the next seat insists
he puts my bag on the rack overhead
though it's heavy and he's old. I let him
and offer a Polo in thanks. He says no,
he's watching his weight and has eaten
two sandwiches for lunch today
when at home he only has soup. He asks where
I'm from. I tell him I used to live
here, where I got on. He says he hears it
in my voice. I smile. Place thickens my throat:
gorse and tor streams. Granite. I tell him
I had to leave and he says so did his daughter.
When she went to university he cried
because he knew she wouldn't come back.
He tells me I'm sounding
right. But when I get where I'm going
people will say I sound like Cwm Rheidol
and slate. I only know sounds, not words.
Here are the sounds of leaving:
newspapers velveting fingers. Curses
for late trains. The coffee machine's hiss.

How to make a good crisp sandwich

For the stranger on the train to Birmingham
who watched but never asked

A ground rule: crisps don't work alone.
They need a baseline, scaffold. Cheese
is ideal. Cheddar, crumbly. Davidstow
as a guide. You need a greaser too.
I go for mayo but butter's fine
or push the boat out with chutney.
Bread must be firm, a day old, two.
It's all about support. Once made, keep
your sandwich open to the light
and the top slice close to hand. Next step
the laying on of crisps. Flavour's
up to you. These are plain – I'm a purist –
but ridged. Think texture. Think noise.
Who does this sandwich want to be?
Distribution's key. Too many and you're just
crunch, sharp edges, salt. Too few
and the hard work's wasted.
When you're satisfied with coverage
grasp the top slice. Don't be timid.
Up turn, plant, then palm-press.
Enjoy the give of crisps. Admire it.
Then you're ready. Both hands.
Take the weight. Lift. You might lose
crisps near the crusts but don't break
your hold. You're committed now.
You have it. It's yours.

Socks or cheese?

You can only have one
for the rest of your life
so the game goes.

Too easy, you think. Losing either
isn't a sacrifice, just shrugging
one off to get on with worrying

about the water bill soon to drain
your wallet. Only later you realise
the seriousness. If picking socks

you'll always be taunted
by feta, begrudge the Cheddar
sandwiches of others. You'll see,

as if there in your living room,
all the cheese you might eat
in a lifetime: Edams

fat as beach balls, reservoirs
of Gruyère, Stilton in buckets.
And if you decide otherwise?

Chaffed in ill-fitting shoes
your feet will weep for love
and remembrance in the snow.

You know your fate:
in the End Days you'll walk
on burning ground,

bare soles blistered to bone
as the last sun sets
on you and your pockets of Brie.

How I know I need a biscuit
in the afternoons

Getting lost in the curtains.
Being almost certain the cats are speaking

English or I am speaking cat.
A need for small spaces:

the airing cupboard, the fridge, a shoebox.
Shouting at the sofa's largesse.

Shutting the shouting in the airing cupboard.
Shoeboxing the sofa's ears.

Hoisting the curtains as sails for a ship
made from the fridge. Press-ganging

the cats for crew to haul anchor for the place
my neighbours whisper I'm bound

when they display their recycling
on Tuesdays. No, don't go –

have some custard creams and climb aboard.
There's always room for one more.

First place

They're only fucking
noises above. We count minutes
shaken by their bed. The fridge

murmurs a soliloquy of ice.
We wake vague, stumbling
into clothes chilled without us

on the floor, once more absurdly
pleased with our damp walls,
the mud creeping from the plughole.

We watch for gifts that send
shadows through the door's frosted
panes: a sherry bottle propped half

full, some unrelated vomit and, once,
a tent that disappeared by lunch.
Last week we sealed the windows

with cling film, keyed it deep
into each sash's gap. The air
has changed; not just warmer now

but thick, and we slow
to suspended animation. We leave
only for milk and to greet the sea,

afraid to be outside for long in case
the cheque has bounced
and parents come to take us home

to stop us playing house.

Bleach

You've burnt me, bleach. Swollen my skin
until it squeaks. I trusted you and took off
my gloves. You left your red stubble touch.

I know you're bad, bleach. I've read your label
and turned from the checkout before now.
I've sworn to give you up for good but

you're so strong, bleach, when it comes
to the mould blooming across my bathroom
and my dreams. I needed you, called out

and you were there, bleach. Still, you must go.
Quick, no one will know. You've chewed my fingers
and swallowed my prints with your stink

so I'm blameless and raw as I tuck you in,
hide your face amongst the softer yet so much
weaker ecological bottles under the sink.

Sirens

Fourteen years old
at the most, stretching

rocket-printed Speedos
and safe over there

in the club's lane. His girls
are flat as tiles, giggling

braces beneath rubber
scalps, all fish-eyed

innocence. Exiles,
we watch his butterfly

arms slice choppy
chlorine. Blood clamours

to the surface, even bone
has a pulse when he rests

at the deep end, back
bared for feasting.

The girls on the train

are laughing so hard they're bawling, broken
by it, might be sick – faces purple
in the joke, sweating their blather and stupid
with laughter and I wonder why
when they're getting off at Borth
for fuck's sake, that Twin Peaks
by the sea, and I hate them because
I've become this Arriva Trains Wales seat –
my early velour glory lost to coffee
stains and strange holes someone's
tried to glue closed and as I watch
the girls tumble to the platform
in a hot heap of themselves
and what they share I see at once
that my writing is the line to Barmouth:
poorly served, subject to frequent delays.

What I saw on my Jubilee weekend trip to London

Two girls on the Victoria Line
opening their bags and tipping
drifts of stolen knickers into
their laps, comparing spoils:
purple lace, orange thongs, sky blue
leopard print, some chintzy briefs.
They sifted them, let them fall
through their hands, the loot
so many silent birds of paradise.

And the shock of my face
in the window. The admiration
caught there. The want.

How the world began

St Mary's R.C. School, year four special project

the nuns brought
                        this word dry
fizzing my tongue:
                        Australia   Aust   ral   ia   Austral   ia

and I was parched and drank it

                                ★

rainbow serpent the nuns said

                                                the dry words

rainbow serpent's people wouldn't say   but their words

weren't mine to use   I can't write them

here   though I was in that classroom   sitting

still in that classroom
the great snake goes on
inching rivers
                        waterholes   veins
        the gullies
of memory making
                        mountains   shifting
years pushing Genesis

                into the dark
all that I remember:

★

a blessing   best pencils to make the world

                 beautiful country:
the moor   the bush

on my page before I said Grace   before I lined up
behind the nuns at break

      before I confessed

            ★

                       forgive me   father
for I have sinned
            it has been lifetimes since
I took what was not mine   am taking
still just listen to this
            white girl dreaming

Brief encounter
with recycling

I don't see you
over the recycling
piled in my arms.

You do your best
to avoid me
but I'm on a mission

to reduce waste
and tend to swerve
in the stairwell.

If this was a film
we'd have to fall in love
but I'm in love

with someone else
who doesn't mind
that I swerve,

someone who rinses
empty juice cartons
before piling them

in his arms
to carry halfway
across town

to the appropriate bin.
The blood on your cheek
from the torn corner

of my cardboard box
is not the stuff
of romance and neither

is your shouting.
I'm not going to take you
for coffee and apologies,

dab your face
with a napkin in an act
of accidental intimacy,

tell you I hate
my boyfriend and long
to escape the stairs

and this life of recycling.
Instead, I'm going to collect
my scattered plastic cups,

crisp packets and poem drafts
and carry on past
your anger, confident

the scene was worth it
in avoiding landfill waste
and knowing that later

the person I love and I
will agree that some people
are just awful.

Red Admiral as teaching aid

Faltering, as if already broken, it wing-limped
through September's dust and honey light, gift
to the kids proving to sleep in the soft oven room
when one boy, bored and beyond me, lifted
an amazed finger and said –
as if it was a charm to pull it to his lips,
as if it was the name of somebody he loved
– *butterfly*.

It stuttered across the ceiling to the strip light
and dropped into its diamond mesh. The patter
was a leaf turning from summer, letting go.

I carried on with the lesson. Poems. They hated them,
hated me, too. When I left there was nothing to see
in the light's box. Perhaps it got out.

My dental hygienist and I listen to Radio 2

I open up. Plaque, he says, and scrapes me.

What colour ribbon did Max tie round the old oak tree?

My teeth are splitting.

We'll have to push you for an answer.

I spit small clots.

Name the first studio album from Oasis.

Polish, like being pebble-dashed. Like dying?

Ok, moving on. Two minutes left.

My tongue flops, is braised by the buzz head.

Who had a number one hit with Breathless?

I am slobber. Shining pain. Finished, he says.

Here's what you got wrong.

Swill, he says. The beach in my mouth.

Would you like to say hi to anyone before you go?

I regret not wearing braces when there was less shame.

Coming up next – travel and weather.

I've seen worse, he says. I swallow the blood.

But first, the song everyone's talking about–

Floss, he says. The answer is to floss.

Raspberries

Why were we at your mother's then?
The visit has slipped its purpose.
All I remember is she asked us to pick
the raspberries lured to ripeness by the rain.
It had been wet all week and I didn't know
what coat to pack.

She was watching, I think, as we limboed
the canes. My elbow cupped
a Christmas pudding shell she had saved.
My mother does the same.

Some berries sighed away, late beads
leaving the hug. Others held
their sour breath and clenched. You told me
the centres looked like hard white hearts.

She was there when we finished and your fingers
were bloodied with juice and fine hairs.
Yes, she laughed as she hung the washing out.

I asked her how she grew the raspberries,
how she globed such sweetness in soft moleskin.
This I know for certain:
she smiled, looked at the sun and said

it was nothing.

Ghazal from John

For JT

Did you know that a leech that eats another leech
will remember all the first leech knew, John asks.

No, the small birds that rootle rock pools by the pier
are in fact striped plovers, John points out.

Drinking during the day is like being born again
after lunch, I think I hear John say.

Dormice don't actually touch the ground. They leap
from tree to tree, like this, John shows me.

Your first go at toad in the hole will live forever
in its failure, John assures me.

Felicity Kendal in dungarees, digging up her homegrown,
makes my heart melt, John murmurs.

Poems bloom in allotments and travel the memory
of leeches. This one is yours, I tell John.

Oi oi axolotls

For Amy McCauley

what are ya like?

ya big smilers
ya pink high-rollers

ya doing ya lack of gravity
tap dance in ya glass tank
at the Chinese while we wait
for our Kung Pao chicken

ya toothy walking fish
bite off a leg and show me
ya great trick – growing back
what's gone

ya know this is it now
axolotl diaspora
even miracles
can't grow homeland

ya still chipper though
all tadpoles cum mini sharks
lungless looking
on the bright side

ya my melted My Little Ponies
swimming for ya lives
love ya babes
love ya

Nightmare at pony camp

Beyond the barn, invisible horses
tore roots and snorted each other's
twitch. Lolling with charred

marshmallows, we yawned
for pony club tales, from bales,
fold-up chairs, a Li Lo.

The teller was a small man, fox-nosed,
pierced, a waist we craved. Teacher
but paperless, whispering his past lives

only to colts. Roll-ups fell limp
with waiting on his lip. We ached
the unsaid, our mothers too

needing truth, not his winks and shuffled
could-be-fibs. They left us, certain our pert
silence would drag his story clear.

She came, he said, like a heart attack
while he dreamt tight dressage, clopping
the boards to heave her bristled bulk

above his face. Her grey tongue learnt
the lay of him, breath huffed molten
the length of his sweating. Silage, drink

and a hint of his sister. She laughed
a broken whinny when he cried, smiled
a trap for snatching early love. We left him

weeping to the straw and gawped out,
past our sleeping mounts, to top field
and tents baring zip grins in the dark.

There's no such thing as pandas

I cut my teeth on *Newsround* where 'And finally'
meant pandas: pandas on planes, panda love
at London Zoo, the Queen unveils a new panda.
There was something about them, even then.
Those tricks-of-a-hypnotist eyes. The big pads
moving like hands. Were they shoes
inside the feet? I wasn't sure until I saw
the sneezing baby make her mother
lurch in shock on YouTube. Then I knew:
pandas are just people in suits, having us on.

Missed you at Cwmdonkin Drive

Today, Dylan, I came for a reading, found you out
so left this poem, to say that I was there, was ready
with my re-cit-ation voice, my pages all crumpled moist

and my hands ashake, today, Dylan, after I roared
cursing round Swansea's one-way system,
my satnav helpless as a goose in a dishwasher

but I got there, Dylan – today, Dylan, had you
forgotten? – up the hill to your green front door
then up the stairs and down again, called your name

but found you out – today! Dylan, you didn't catch
my moment in the front room, the good room,
as I hymned from the chaise-longue, eyeing the brass,

the rug, the spick-span fender. Today, Dylan, I sang
my own song, my not quite all grown song – a seagull
yarking at the dado rail – but I wanted you

and your voice, today. Dylan, your strange notes
wouldn't chime with mine but still we could sing
of waiting and thinking and the words that come

in the night and the morning and today, Dylan –
these words, this song. I came to nose about,
poke about, turn about in your house and your life

and I found this today, Dylan, while you were out.

Hospitality

Come, friend, and toast my return
to these whitewashed shingle shores
and a table straining with my good fortune:
stuffed clams and fat half-shells,
bottlenecks choked with cream
and a well-fleshed woman waiting.

I set the pineapple at the window
for welcome, and to show my dear wife's
not a widow yet. See how she smashes
the lobster and guts the sprats – her wrists
are the quarryman's desire.

I'll be back at sea before
the spiked crown pales with dust,
before its barrel belly softens and curls.
The fruit will be as butter when I go,
so fresh the juice will sticky-drip from
my wife's chin.
               That thought alone
could tempt a man to shuck his work

but Missus must have her larder stocked.
It won't be long until she puts another fruit
on the sill for I will cross the Meridian
and round the horn back to my wife-warm bed
while your crops are still to turn.

Friend, don't you envy me?

Here, take the glass. I'll show you
the lass that keeps me away:
a fine girl, stout and well-built
in oak and hard-driven rivets.
She lounges beyond the bluff
safe from the cheek of wind
seeking to scupper a landed man.

In her hold lie riches branded
with my mark: tea, spice, slaves
trained to free any weed-bound soil
including your dry acre.
Wasn't this our dream,
to have others do our bidding?

As children at our fathers' knees, those farmers
creaking toil and disappointment,
we planned routes to riches on the trade winds.
We were to master men, sail mapless
on seas we knew like lovers.

Yet you leave me on the waves
alone. Those curséd wheat ears keep you still.

Don't you wish at least to have a woman
of your own? My wife cooks well
and doesn't pull my purse strings.
Isn't she a catch? I miss her so
I cannot speak at times.
                              Such rot
I bore you with! Drink up –

When May comes

I'll miss the pigeon that daily batters
the berried tree by my window.

She's a busty girl, dips thin branches
with a ruffle when she sits.

She likes things out of
reach, tilting beak beneath tail

to lunge upside down, a parrot
in post-war grey. She is jerky

as Chaplin, always at the point
of falling but never quite.

Sometimes she hits the glass like she's
breaking into this room that won't

be mine when May comes.
There – see how she's looking

right at me, wing raised in a sail
for balance, for making me see.

Don't get comfortable, she says.
Don't bother lining your nest.

Albatross dance

On the island there is time to learn
the steps again, to remember how sound wears
at rock in a storm of beaks shrieking romance.
At first, the signs are loose and prodigals flap
dumb to the edge. But each must find their only half.
Sometimes chance, sometimes fate throws in
an encounter on a ledge, a branch just
so, and so it begins. His wings hinge gangles
and rain, his feet web an atlas of love –
all the down before her. Enamoured eye-
to-eye they duck and docey-doe, shoot
pole-necks and clack to the other's heart.
Weaving whips them up until the furthest span
feathers the light and tips brush, then blur.
Divorce is rare but widows crowd. He leaves her
sharpened kisses, shells as strong as cliffs.

Paragliders off Pen Dinas

Come with me on Sunday and we'll see them tear
down the footpath's loose shale so fast

you'll think they're going to end it *en masse.*
You'll shout for them to stop, tell them life

can't be that bad, but they'll ignore you and jump
for the sea. Technicolour will blossom

from nothing behind them and you'll suck
your hysteria in like it's air and you're drowning.

Even seagulls will be shocked to shyness,
scything mutely past the big lips

that kiss the hill with shadows.
Beneath them sexless swathes of harness will hang,

still as the dead. There is some devil pact
with updraughts keeping them in giddy silence

for quick-slow quick-slow turns that never quite
bring them down.

All you'll hear for days is silk: silk snagging
the wind, silk crumpling like paper, silk smothering skin.

In your dreams you'll lie heavy as a lodestone,
crying to join them and leave me behind.

Brian Blessed in Pwllheli

SciFi Weekender, 2013

Brian takes to the stage
for what's meant to be a Q&A
about Flash Gordon and his love
of goosing but he's
on a mission to spread
the good word
about space:
        we are children
of stardust, meant to travel further
than thought, the moon
only the start:
        Mars, Jupiter, Saturn are waiting
for us who must leap light years now.

Brian announces he's completed
cosmonaut training and is ready
to go. He holds out his hand and I,
until now afraid
of space –
     the cold, the ease
          of getting lost and my head
             exploding –
take it. The hall's sticky carpet
and discarded Starbucks cups
melt away as I mount the stage
and Brian's saying yes, yes, that's it
and the walls fall flat and the floor
warms then lifts and we're going
            going
              gone.

Canada

I've never seen you.
In my head you run from me
in a spool: winter lakes pining for night,
blackened snow, muddy as shadow.
No one comes. In the heart of your forest I beat
my hands on rock, on the bone of land
I've never seen. You

run the heart, but not bone.
No one comes. The forest is black
and muddies rock. Shadows never beat
my head but in winter. I've seen pines spooling
night from your land like snow.
The lakes are my hands
running into the heart, into bone

though winter snows the lakes
to rock. In the black forest
heartbeats spool shadows. Do you
see? No one comes. Night
and the bones in the pines run muddy.
My head is never a land inside
though winter snows. Lake

forest, keep running
into the land shadowed by my head.
You spool rock and bone-
beaten hearts. I see pines snow-muddy
the black of the lakes.
No one comes. Never. Winter
is the forest keep. Running,

no one comes.
Pool to see my heart, bones, hands
beaten by the land and the lakes and the rocks
and the pines and the snow I've never seen.
At night, shadowed muddy, black as winter,
your forest runs my head.
No one comes.

I decided to have a night out

Cooee the fireworks flared
to me on the bridge.
Look look rockets

whistled and smashed.
Boy racer tyres squealed
fuck you back.

I worried for the cats
who hate fireworks
and loud boys.

I've had enough,
I thought and tongued
a stray spark, swallowing

the bang. Cinders
warmed my slip
into the river shifty

as an eel, put bulbs
in my eyes to dodge
shopping trolleys

and get straight out to sea.
There I found the moon
buoyed by waves

like a cake on a tray.
I ate that too.
America was a long way.

Cold

when you reach for me
    I am glacier
        dragging rocks and bone

I am mountains
    silenced by drifts
        of packed snow

I am buried too deep
    for melt water
        when you reach for me

because in the mountains
    there are men so cold
        they think they are warm

so cold they dream
    another's hand reaching
        for them in the hurting dark

when you reach for me
    I am avalanche
        and they are already dead

Geography lesson

I was learning ice, the creep
of a glacier if I turned away, how it poured

from the névé supple as cream
but was slow-witted and a hoarder of scree.

I remember the video flickering seizures
to show, beneath the crust of the terminus, eyes

in a puddle of skin, a head steam-rollered
flat. His nose and mouth had slipped

past an ear. Teeth lay scattered in his hair.
His eyebrows had escaped.

Innocence gave him away:
tweed knickerbockers and a woollen coat

left a date but not a name. The voiceover said
the man had travelled a hundred years,

as if the day he set out, kissing
a long dead love, clearing his throat

with a good sharp bark, checking
his map once more for inky warnings

of weak ice, as if that day
hadn't ended with his fall.

The trip thinned him
to paper but he was as pink

as if he'd just that moment gasped
the pure air of the crevasse

and longed to speak the shock
still spreading across his face.

Spook of the Antarctic

Captain Scott
is a hide sleeping bag
battered by the tent's flap
and the wind wringing his baby son's name.

Captain Scott
has frostbite lips. His kiss
burns feet, fingers, faces.
He casts no shadow in the night-time sun.

Captain Scott
has glass eyes. Hood man
hairless, stink of burnt tallow.
He is an oil slick and fat as a seal.

Captain Scott
is Bowers, Evans, and Oates' sad
one-liner. Bad luck
loves him as it waltzes to the pole.

Captain Scott
hasn't died. He sees my sins
and weeps inside the ice. One day
he'll make it to the sea again   and then

Royal icing

It brought me back to land, that cake, kept me months
in galleys that didn't pitch, didn't fill with heaving men.
Training had whipped my ambition, stirred a need
for swift precision, and the blueprint proved in dreams.

Rum-drenched fruit foundations, cement of yolks
and sugar joists. It would be tall but not as tall as her:
I want a cake, not a monument. But I couldn't stop.

Each sultana had to pass eight separate checks.
Cherries only made it if they glowed.
The icing took me weeks to roll; a growing fall
of snow it settled fast then drank all light nearby.

She looked afraid, her smile lost
inside the white. I saw it later as I covered cracks
with fresh caresses.
                    Too much hid in that blinding place:
my father's voice, torn football cards, the allotment
after dark.

People only ask me now because
she's dead, as if the recipe has answers.
How many raisins? How many eggs?

Acknowledgements

Thanks are due to the editors of the following publications, in which some of the poems in this collection first appeared: *The Cadaverine, Cheval* anthologies for the Terry Hetherington Prize (Parthian, 2012, 2013, 2014), *The Factory, James Dickey Review, The Lampeter Review, Magma, New Welsh Review, Planet, Poetry Wales, Newspaper Taxis: Poetry After the Beatles* (Seren, 2013).

'Telescope' was the Honno poem of the month for October 2012 and appeared on their website.

'Swine Song' was a runner up in the inaugural *New Welsh Review* poetry competition in 2009.

'Royal Icing' (previously entitled 'Snow-blind') won the 2011 Leaf Books Poetry Competition.

I would like to thank my teachers, colleagues and friends in the Department of English and Creative Writing at Aberystwyth University, then and now, for their insightful advice and support over many years, and without whom this book would not exist: Maria Apichella, Tiffany Atkinson, Katy Birch, Creina Francis, Matthew Francis, Kelly Grovier, Amy McCauley, Richard Marggraf Turley, Kevin Mills, Jem Poster and Damian Walford Davies. I am grateful, too, for the support of Samantha Wynne-Rhydderch and Phillip Gross. Thank you to my wonderful editor, Amy Wack, and everyone at Seren. Thank you to my family.

Well chosen words

Seren is an independent publisher with a wide-ranging list which includes poetry, fiction, biography, art, translation, criticism and history. Many of our books and authors have been on longlists or shortlists for - or won - major literary prizes, among them the Costa Award, the Man Booker, the Desmond Elliott Prize, The Writer's Guild Award, Forward Prize, and TS Eliot Prize.

At the heart of our list is a beautiful poem or a good story told well or an idea or history presented interestingly or provocatively. We're international in authorship and reader-ship though our roots are here in Wales (Seren means Star in Welsh), where we prove that writers from a small country with an intricate culture have a worldwide relevance.

Our aim is to publish work of the highest literary and artis-tic merit that also succeeds commercially in a competitive, fast changing environment. You can help us achieve this goal by reading more of our books – available from all good bookshops and increasingly as e-books. You can also buy them at 20% discount from our website, and get monthly updates about forthcoming titles, readings, launches and other news about Seren and the authors we publish.

www.serenbooks.com